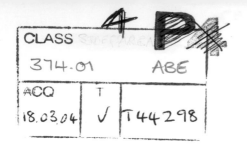
> "*Ability to reconstitute words can unquestionably be improved by training and practice*"
> (M. Peters)

Acknowledgements

I would like to thank the following establishments for the use of their worksheets throughout the publication: Harlow College, ABE Open Learning Centre, Colchester and ABE Scheme, Thurrock.

ISBN 1 870741 74 9

Design: Studio 21

First edition published February 1994

Reprinted July 1995

Second reprint November 1997

Third reprint February 2000

Contents

1. About Spelling   5

A.   The spelling process

B.   Implications for the student

C.   Implications for the tutor

D.   Attitudes to spelling

E.   Who needs to spell correctly?

F.   What do you need to know about your student?

G.   Improving spelling – the sequence

H.   The place of spelling in the curriculum

I.   Developing the programme

J.   A contract for developing better spelling

K.   Approaches to spelling

L.   A check list for assessment

M.   Looking at student writing

N.   Responding to student writing

O.   Responding to spelling mistakes

P.   Crucial errors

Q.   Diagnosing spelling strengths and needs

R.   Negotiating the curriculum

S.   Lesson planning

T.   A weekly action plan for improving spelling

U.   Practise, practise, practise

V.   How do you spell this?

W.   The vocabulary of spelling

X.   Independent learning

Y.   Recording spellings

Z.   Testing

2. Helping your Student to Spell – Teaching and learning spelling, do's and dont's 36

A. The visual approach
   1. Look, See, Cover, Imagine, Write, Check, Practise
   2. Looking attentively at words
   3. Flash cards
   4. Games
   5. Words within words
   6. Discrimination

B. Developing skills of visualisation
   1. Look, Cover, Write, Check
   2. Games
   3. Cloze

C. The auditory approach
   1. Sound to letter correspondence
   2. Doubling
   3. Pronunciation
   4. Groups of words

D. Kinaesthetic approaches
   1. Handwriting

E. Logical
   1. Syllables
   2. Meaningful letter strings – morphemes
   3. Root words
   4. Prefixes
   5. Suffixes
   6. Tense discrimination
   7. Meanings
   8. The history lesson
   9. Rules
   10. Imaginative approaches

3. The Role of Dictation 63

4. Spelling and Accreditation 65

5. Aids and Resources 67

6. Using and Choosing a Dictionary 73

7. Special Problems 78

8. Sample Worksheet 83

9. Summary: What the Curriculum Needs to Include 85

1 | About Spelling

A. The spelling process

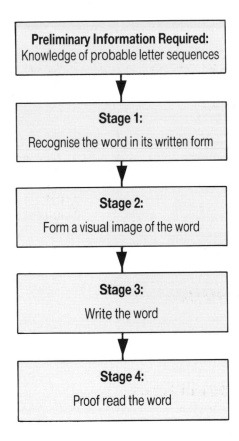

Preliminary Information Required:
Knowledge of probable letter sequences

Stage 1:
Recognise the word in its written form

Stage 2:
Form a visual image of the word

Stage 3:
Write the word

Stage 4:
Proof read the word

This process may appear very simple but it is only through a thorough understanding and application of it that you can effectively help those who wish to improve their spelling. The process needs to be mirrored in the methods and materials which you use. Students also need to understand the process so that they are able to make decisions leading to positive outcomes.

B. Implications for the student

The student needs to:

Have learned

- a coding system based on the probabilities of letters occuring in certain sequences in English.

Know

- as much as possible about the English language
- several strategies for learning spelling
- where to look for help.

Be able to

- read
- visualise a word once seen
- get thoughts down on paper
- proof read
- check spellings in reference works.

Feel

- that spelling is only a tool for writing
- confident that spelling can be improved
- willing to **practise, practise, practise.**

C. Implications for the tutor

It follows that the tutor must teach:

- knowledge of English letter strings, most specifically those required immediately by the student and therefore most likely to be *used* by the student.
- a range of methods for remembering
- visualisation
- proof reading
- writing skills – either handwriting or using wordprocessing
- attentive behaviour (that is, **noticing** the features of language).

Therefore the teacher needs:

- knowledge of
  - the spelling process
  - the English language
  - English orthography and how it has evolved.
- skills of
  - diagnosis
  - assessment
  - presentation
  - review
  - evaluation
  - fostering student independence
- to have
  - a positive attitude towards the English spelling system
  - strategies for fostering student independence
  - a structured approach
- to be aware of resources which will help the learner (**and** the teacher).

D. Attitudes to spelling

Many adults in Britain feel unhappy with their spelling.
It is likely that the students you are working with come into this category.
Why is spelling perceived as a problem by so many adults?

The way words are spelt is a reflection of the culture of a language and those who don't spell accurately sometimes feel that they may be regarded as less cultured than those who do.

Spelling is seen as an indication of status and education. Those who are not good at spelling often feel embarrassed about their lack of skill and are unhappy about allowing others to see what they have written. They may even be reluctant to write at all.

> **"I sifted the replies and those that had spelling mistakes went to the bottom of the pile."**
> – From a letter in the Independent, 15.9.93.

Incorrect spellings that are not seen by others are no problem. Some writers may not mind others seeing spelling mistakes which they have made. But most people who think others may see their writing are concerned about making mistakes. Most students you meet will come into that category. Some may have been directed to receive support even though they themselves have not identified their spelling as a problem. This handbook will mainly address the ways in which tutors can help students who believe that they need to improve their spelling.

E. Who needs to spell correctly?

This includes a wide variety of people.

- young people who have recently left school and who may be on training courses where spelling difficulties are a disadvantage

- college students who discover that their spelling is weak when they have to produce written course work

- adults who find that they need to spell accurately for the purpose of specific employment

- unemployed adults who realise that accurate spelling may improve their chances of making a good impression in job applications

- students of English who have been educated with spelling systems very different from the English one (ESOL students)

- adults who just want to spell better.

These students may have come along specifically for spelling, for more general development of literacy skills or as part of a course which they feel they will complete more successfully if they improve their spelling.

F. What do you need to know about your student?

It is likely that you will have contact with your student for very few hours each week so you will want to have clear ideas about how best to help them. In order to do so you will need to discover:

- why they want to improve their spelling

- what they are hoping to gain from learning

- what previous help they have had

- what they already know about spelling

- what strengths they have in spelling

- what strategies they use when they want to learn how to spell a word

- how they feel about spelling

- what sort of spelling difficulties they have
- whether they recognise their own errors.

How can you find the answers to these questions?

- If you normally work with a group of students who all want to improve spelling, you could initiate a group discussion and then later make a note of comments made. **But** – you have to be confident that you aren't going to embarrass any of them or put them on the spot.

- You could ask students to complete a questionnaire. **But** – you have to be aware that those with spelling difficulties may well not feel confident about filling one in.

- You could discuss these questions individually with students. **But** – you need to be aware of giving the impression that spelling difficulties are something to be hidden or ashamed of.

- You'll certainly need to see some writing that the student has done.

G. Improving spelling – the sequence

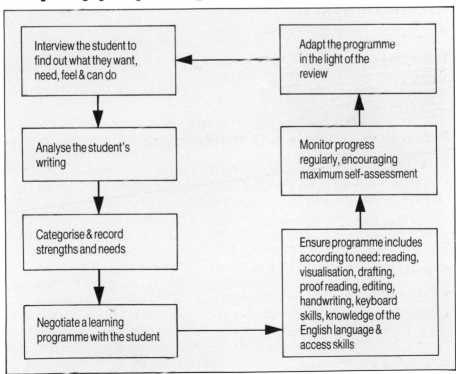

H. The place of spelling in the curriculum

Spelling is of two kinds:

- Absolutely accurate, letter for letter precision which relies on the speller having seen the word before and being able to remember exactly how it looks.

- A good reliable guess based upon knowledge of the language and familiarity with similar words.

You cannot ensure that your student works on or even sees all the words they might want to spell in the future. So you need to help your student to acquire the second type of spelling where they can make a good prediction of how an unfamiliar word might be spelt. You will also need to help your students to use dictionaries and other reference works so that they can check spellings for themselves.

There are a few students who wish to improve their spelling and have no need of any other support or skills development. Such students may need to follow a short straightforward learning programme which concentrates solely on spelling; they are in a minority of adults who want to improve their spelling.

Most need and want to do so in conjunction with the development of associated literacy skills, particularly writing. You are likely then to want and need to offer help with spelling as part of a wider learning programme. This book primarily addresses the issue of helping with spelling but you are likely to need to incorporate that help skilfully into a wider curriculum.

But that is an advantage, not a disadvantage. Spelling is only necessary as part of writing. Students who do not write, do not need to spell and students who will not write are unlikely to get very far with improving spelling. It may be an unpalatable fact but spelling, like any other skill which requires physical and mental co-ordination, requires lots of practice.

Part of the skill of the tutor is in weaving opportunities and requirements for practice into the wider programme and persuading the student to do the same in the context of home, work, etc.

The student who seeks help with spelling may never become a proficient speller but it would be inappropriate for them to continue receiving educational support for their spelling on a permanent basis. This means that student and tutor must have a shared end point in view – a realistic target to aim for which, when achieved, is the agreed springboard for further development or is accepted as an end in itself and should terminate the specific learning contract. If this is so students will need to continue to improve their spelling after they have ceased to receive educational support. An important part of their learning programme therefore is developing independence, confidence and an eagerness to go on learning, as well as a system for doing so.

This needs to colour all contact with the student, whose independence should constantly be fostered. However, you as the tutor will know much more than your student about ways of improving spelling and will need to give advice and information which will enable the student to make productive decisions.

I. Developing the programme

The programme that you work out with the student needs to be:

Relevant

Off-the-shelf books and worksheets may well play a part but should only be used where they address the types of error which your student actually makes or where they introduce or promote practices which address the student's particular difficulties. They also need to coincide with the students' interests as far as possible.

Paced appropriately

The amount of work which the student will realistically complete in the time available and the level of work which is compatible with the students' learning strengths and weaknesses will dictate how much can be expected. This pace might be increased as the student develops confidence, motivation and skills. For many students starting a spelling programme, a few new words to learn each week will probably be as much as they can manage.

Embedded in the curriculum

Spelling is likely to be only a part of what your student wants to achieve. You'll need to work out an acceptable balance which gives sufficient opportunity for feedback and practice of spelling whilst not dominating the curriculum. It is important that spelling is always seen as a tool to enable the student to communicate effectively.

Multi-sensory

It's very important that the student develops an approach which incorporates a wide range of techniques for learning spellings. They need to include:

- **Visual**
- **Auditory**
- **Kinaesthetic**
- **Logical**
- **Semantic.**

Structured

It's easy just to follow the errors in pieces of student writing. But though this provides a starting point it doesn't replace structured planning which ensures that:

- **long term objectives** are identified
- these are based on thorough **assessment** of the students' strengths and weaknesses
- **session plans** work systematically towards the **long term objectives** which have been identified

- each session is **evaluated** and the insights gained from evaluation incorporated into planning

- each session uses a **variety** of methods and approaches

- sessions are interspersed with structured opportunities for **practice** which direct the student towards building up skills outside of class contact time

- **self-assessment** and **self-checking** are built in to promote student independence.

J. A contract for developing better spelling

You will need to make it clear to students that though you can help them improve their spelling they will need to put in a great deal of hard work and frequent practice. Unless they are willing to put in the effort and the time it is unlikely that they will improve. You need to be very frank about this.

Before you embark on the spelling programme make an agreement with each student. The agreement which you make will be of an individual nature but might include some of the features listed below.

The student will:

- identify words they need to learn

- look out for words which fit the current learning pattern

- do some writing between class contact sessions

- practise the words which have been selected for current learning

- practise the method which has been selected and give feed back to you

- provide a dictionary

- provide a notebook

- record new words and patterns in the notebook

- adhere to the programme of contact that has been agreed.

The tutor will:

- identify existing spelling skills which each student has

- find out as far as possible what type of errors the student makes

- negotiate a learning plan with the student

- structure a program based on existing skills and needs

- help the student to select methods of assessing progress

- specify dates for review
- review progress on a regular basis as agreed with the student
- find out as much as possible about spelling in order to give the student maximum support.

K. Approaches to spelling

You probably don't remember learning to spell but if you are going to be involved in teaching spelling it's important that you are aware of the many strategies that adults may use when they need to spell a word.

- They may shut their eyes and try to remember what it looks like.
- They may sound it out slowly to try to identify the different parts of it.
- They may write several versions down until they find one they like the look of.
- They may think about what it means.
- They may think of other words which are similar.
- They may ask one or two trusted people.
- They may use a dictionary or newspaper.

Students may attempt any of these or other ways of trying to recollect a spelling. It is important to know what students prefer and whether they are more effective in using a particular approach.
Students are likely to be more successful if they can use several approaches.

L. A check list for assessment

You will need to record:

- Your students' writing habits:
  - what do they write?
  - for what purpose?
  - under what conditions?
- Do they use a dictionary? If so, which one? and how?
- Do they use technological aids such as computer, wordprocessor, spell checks?
- Together you will need to set specific targets which are realistically achievable within an agreed time scale.

The targets should include specific words or types of words but should also identify some learning techniques that will help. They also need to indicate the time scale which has been agreed. They will also need to include specified amounts of writing practice.

Some possible targets:

- *In a passage of my own writing I can successfully spot most of the errors which I make.*

- *When I spot one of my own spelling errors I can usually tell which bits are wrong.*

- *When I have identified a wrongly spelt bit of a word I can think of likely possible alternatives.*

- *I have increased my knowledge of the English language by . . .*

- *I can use . . . . different strategies for remembering how words are spelt.*

- *I can look up words in the dictionary to see if I have spelt them correctly.*

- *I have learned 'x' number of spellings which are necessary to me.*

M. Looking at student writing

First students need to understand their place in identifying spelling strengths and needs. They also need to know that you can only help with spelling if you can look at a piece of writing which the student has done and which contains spelling mistakes. This means encouraging students to use words which they would like to use even if they are not sure how to spell them. It is helpful if they are willing to guess or predict, it is therefore crucial that you establish a culture which values mistakes. You need to say that the students who will learn are those who are not afraid to take risks and make mistakes.

- You will need to be sure that your student understands why this is so.

- The least stressful way of achieving it may be to use an existing piece of the student's writing. It is likely that your student will be doing writing activities as part of a wider learning programme. Spelling needs to fit into this as unobtrusively as possible.

- If nothing already exists you will need to get the student to write something. As far as possible it should be something which they might really want to write, rather than a task which has been concocted specifically for assessment purposes.

- If your student has difficulty thinking of a writing task you may need to devise something which is relevant to their situation, e.g. filling in a form, writing a letter of application, a letter to a friend, an essay, etc. It must be stressed they are to draft only.

N. Responding to student writing

Once you have a piece of student writing it is very important that you:

- Ask the student to read it to you if this is possible. This pre-empts you having to ask the student to help you with reading mis-spelled words you can't understand.

- Read it.

- React to it positively as communication.

- Ask the student to comment on the writing.

- Comment on the content.

- Give some positive reaction.

- Ask your student to read it through to see if they can spot any words wrongly spelt. If they manage to find any, give them praise for the successful proof reading.

- Note down some of the incorrect spellings that have been identified. This needs to be done systematically *(see Diagnosing Strengths and Weaknesses, page no.18)*.

- Record and analyse the errors made.

- Praise correct spellings of some words.

Hopefully the student will have had specific purposes in mind in writing the piece and you will want to address the question of how far the writing satisfies the student's purposes before going on to look at surface features of the writing:

- Does the passage express the intended meaning?

- Are the words the ones which the student wanted to use?

- Can the student think of any better way of expressing what they want to say?

- Is the piece laid out to the best effect?

- How effective is the piece for its intended audience?

Only then will you want to direct your student's attention to possible spelling errors. Remember, it's important that students initially undertake the proof reading themselves.

Are there any words in the passage which the student thinks might be spelt incorrectly? These could be indicated in an appropriate way, highlighter pen, underlining, etc. It is in everyone's best interest if the student only finds a few – 5 or less is best. If the student finds as many as that it will depend upon the purpose of the writing whether you point out any more. If it's a classroom piece and not for anyone else's eyes there is no particular virtue in directing the student's attention towards so many errors that they can't effectively be dealt with in the immediate future.

However, the student may have spotted errors which don't seriously impede comprehension whilst ignoring errors which are much more crucial. In this case it will be necessary to point out the errors whose correction will most enhance the writing. In any case you'll want to record the types of error for your planning.

You will also want the student to record the types of error which they habitually make so that they can see the relevance of the approaches which you suggest.

Students who write on a word processor will probably become used to using a spell check but they will need to be aware that spell check won't pick up any words used incorrectly but which are nevertheless words (e.g. wear/where).

If the student has not made any errors (it does happen!) you'll need to discover whether they have deliberately chosen a simple piece of writing to avoid errors or whether the spelling problem is more perceived than real. If the former, they will need to be encouraged to tackle a piece of writing which is more likely to reveal weaknesses.

If the student has made few errors and identifies them all, you will probably use the words mis-spelt in devising an initial learning programme.

If the student identifies few errors but has made many you will need to decide which errors are crucial ones.

O. Responding to spelling mistakes

It is best if the student has spotted the error themselves. If you have spotted the error after they have proof read the student should always be given the correct written version and asked to check against their own version. If they can't spot discrepancies you will need to underline or highlight in some way until the student **notices** the discrepancy.

They then need some insights into **why** they made the error and **why** the word is spelt as it is. This is where your knowledge of the language and your knowledge of the student enables you to make use of the error as a springboard for the student's learning and development.

You will want to follow it up by pointing out words which share the same pattern, particularly if it is one which has already cropped up in previous work.

You will of course react differently to spelling mistakes according to the student's writing purposes and the learning contract which you have made with them. If they are writing a creative piece to express their thoughts and opinions on a particular subject, or if they are writing a long and very detailed report where content is of primary importance you may feel that spelling mistakes can remain. However, if the student's writing is to be seen and judged in any way by others you will probably point out every error.

16

P. Crucial errors

Most people make some spelling mistakes at some time. That doesn't need to be a problem. But if spelling errors:

- make it difficult to understand a piece of writing
- give an impression of sloppiness or lack of skill
- make a piece of writing look bad
- prevent the writer achieving their objectives

– they become crucial and need to be addressed.

Any writer might make different types of error in the same piece of writing. Which errors are crucial depend on the student's specific situation. For each person who writes there is a personally important vocabulary. For most of us it usually starts with our name and address. If we're out of work it includes the language we want to use in writing job applications. If we are in employment it may be the words which are related to specific tasks which we need to perform. For the chair of the fancy pigeon society it may be the names of pigeon breeds that are most crucial. Students on college courses may well need to acquire the specific vocabulary of a craft such as carpentry or catering. It follows that you the tutor must know which words are crucial words for each of your students.

Assessment sheet for spelling	never	sometimes	always
Words which I consistently spell correctly			
Letter groups which I consistently spell correctly			
Techniques which I know for remembering spellings			
I write (list examples of writing to be done)			
I can spot my own mistakes			
When I spot mistakes I can make a good attempt at putting them right			
I record the words which I have learned			
I record letter groups which I have learned			

Q. Diagnosing spelling strengths and needs

Why is diagnosis important?

In order to ensure that the learning programme addresses the needs of the individual student effectively, it is vital that the programme is based upon a thorough assessment which should include a careful diagnosis of the student's spelling behaviour. From this it will be much easier for you to ensure that the precious moments of contact time are used in ways which address the spelling problems, build on the student's strengths and result in development and progression.

Who should undertake the diagnosis?

In order to help your student become a good speller you will need to know a great deal about the spelling process and about the English writing system. This knowledge enables you to 'see' the patterns of spelling which your student is using and to categorise them so that you can then devise a directly relevant learning programme.

You will need to negotiate the programme with each student. But there is no point in students continuing to use methods and approaches which have failed them in the past and are likely to fail them in the future even if they express a liking for them.

Later on in the programme as students increase their knowledge of spelling and acquire study habits which promote skills development they will be able to contribute more to the partnership. But in the early stages of the learning programme you will need to undertake this diagnostic role.

How should diagnosis take place?

You will need to base your diagnosis partly on the student's writing. It is important that you note the spelling patterns which the student uses successfully as well as noting all errors. You will then need to categorise the errors made. The categories often used for spelling errors are:

	example
• **Omissions**	bother/brother
• **Contractions**	rember/remember
• **Insertions**	pretened/pretend
• **Transpositions**	grils/girls
• **Doubling**	seatting/seating
• **Substitution**	possiply/possibly
• **Homophones**	wear/where
• **Perseverations**	belongonging/belonging

18

You will want a simple system for recording strengths and weaknesses on a regular basis. One of the simplest ways is to devise a diagnostic sheet. The diagnostic sheet which you devise for your own student only needs to include the types of error which they actually make. It is often desirable, therefore, to agree terminology with your student for categories of error which they are making. *(see example No. 1)*. If they are making a great many different types of error it is important also to record the spelling patterns which they habitually reproduce correctly. These can then be used to boost their confidence and as a way into successful spelling of words which use similar patterns.

You will probably want to enable your student to take an active part in the diagnosis.

Your diagnosis also needs to include an analysis of your student's **attempts** at spelling. You may decide to use a dictation so that you can observe the student at the writing task. If you devise a piece for dictation it should be based on the student's own words and language.

If you are teaching more than one student you will need to observe patterns of error on a wider basis and will need diagnostic sheets which record the errors made by a number of people. These will assist in your planning, particularly in steering the balance of individual and group activity. *(see Example No.2)*.

When should diagnosis be undertaken?

Once you have established what sort of writing your student wants to do and with what frequency, you will need to decide what kind of records it would be appropriate to keep. It is important to diagnose the errors in your student's writing but it may not be feasible to deal with every piece systematically.

If few samples are available they would all be marked using the diagnostic sheets which you have devised. A summary of the information on the sheets would then be incorporated into your assessment.

If students write a great quantity you will want to deal diagnostically with regular samples.

If students need to write for diverse purposes – job applications and creative writing for example – you will be encouraging a very different approach to spelling in each of these contexts and will also act upon your diagnosis differently.

Diagnostic sheets of this kind are for constant reference and updating by you and your student. You will have agreed review dates for periodic re-assessment but the diagnostic sheets should guide all your planning.

For diagnostic purposes you need to analyse as far as possible the **reasons** for spelling errors made in student writing.

For such an analysis to be of maximum use it needs to be based on a great many errors. In the early stages you will probably have to base your diagnosis on few.

Your knowledge of the spelling process will help you.

Example No.1.

Types of spelling error	Example	Should have been	Method for learning	Evaluation	Testing
I missed out a vowel					
I missed out a consonant					
I added a vowel					
I added a consonant					
I put in a word which sounds like					

Example No.2

DIAGNOSTIC SHEET FOR CLASS USE (PAGE 1)

Type	Example	Who	Diagnosis	Action	Evaluation
Omissions	-ed	Maria, Montse, Douglas	Spanish? " Hearing?	• Tenses • Proof-reading • Discrimination	OCT All three can do the discrim-ination but still miss out when free writing and proof-reading • gap filling?
	shing, shring, passin, Passing	Douglas, Mary	Hearing? Hearing Attention?	Whole class? • Auditory discrimination	
	tuen, thuiy, Stranger, Stranges	Douglas "		• Letter stringing Douglas, Maria, Montse	NOV Seems to be working Fewer examples BUT CONTINUE PROOF-READING
Phonic Alternative	whare, whare, their, thare, spesk, spesk, cheater, cheetah, sertain	Matthew, Carol, Matthew, Carol, Matthew	Seems to have had too much Phonic teaching	✱ LCWC • letter string here, where, etc • words within words Whole class?	OCT Both Matt and Carol show improvement now using more difficult words NOV-Carol still on phonics ✱ VISUAL METHOD-give her some extra homework
Substitute	Tapestuy, amethush, amethyst	Matthew, Barry	Sounding out again Sounding out?	• Letter string try • Occupation words-try Matthew ✱ Origins of words Whole-class	OCT-Matthew is writing much more BUT • PROOFREADING-need to do more of this with whole class

21

The errors will be due to:

• Lack of **knowledge** of serial probability of English	qiet for quiet
• Lack of noticing the **visual** features of the word	propte/property
• Lack of **visualisation** skills	rember/remember
• Faulty **auditory** discrimination	settle/settled
• Confusion through rules or generalisation	where/wear
• Interference from previous learning	fation/fashion

R. Negotiating the curriculum

The content and methodology of your teaching sessions need to be negotiated with the student, but students can only make meaningful decisions on the basis of knowledge and of confidence. You will have to be ready to guide the student towards decisions which will give them the best chance of achieving, their objectives. You can only do this if you have a thorough knowledge of the students need to write, their writing habits, their attitude and the strategies they are already using. You also need to note the nature of the errors which they make and any specific learning difficulties or perceptual problems encountered.

Such information needs to be recorded systematically for immediate and future use. It is important that the student and tutor together agree on learning targets. This agreement may take the form of an **action plan** *(see example on page 24)*. You may already be familiar with action plans. They need to record the student's writing skills and the difficulties the student has identified as being important.

At all stages and with all processes encourage the student to take as much control as possible. Students should feel that their action plans belong to them and therefore need to determine the content and thrust of the plan as well as the pacing which is agreed.

S. Lesson planning

Having diagnosed the developmental needs of your student in relation to spelling and negotiated what is to be included in the curriculum, you will need to plan the content and methodology of each lesson. These will depend on frequency, timing and the numbers of students you are teaching but it is likely that each lesson will include the following components:

• **Feedback** on homework. This needs to take account of the writers own perceptions before incorporating the views of other class members (if appropriate) and those of the teacher.

- **Identification** of aspects of writing which need development.

- **Identification** of words and letter strings which should form the basis of future spelling work.

- **Practising, Testing, Checking, Reviewing**.

- **Planning, Negotiating** of future work.

- **Oral** activities and interaction.

- **Reading** activities.

- **Writing** stimulation.

- **Writing** activities.

- **Teaching** or **Rehearsing** of methods for learning spellings.

- **Dictionary** work.

- **Language** work.

- **Group** activities if you have more than one student.

- **Homework** setting.
  This could be:
  - to identify needs which occur in student's lives **or**
  - develop work done in class **or**
  - preparation for future class or homework **or**
  - to develop study skills **or**
  - to develop independence **or**
  - to inculcate habits of writing **or**
  - to provide a purpose for writing **or**
  - **any other purpose agreed between you**.

TERMLY ACTION PLAN

Review dates:

Interim ....

End of term ....

Agreed

Name ....

Tutor ....

Date ....

What I want to achieve	**When**
I want to be able to write without worrying about my spelling.	eventually.

The steps I am going to take	**When**
I will do my homework	every week
I will do some spelling	"
I will learn 5 new spellings	"
I will practice a new way of learning spellings	"

My tutor will	**When**
Set me some homework	every week
Mark my homework	"
Give me advice	"
Give me a spelling test	"
Give me a dictation	"
Teach me a new technique for learning spelling	"

Writing I will do	**When**
A letter	by Christmas
A book review	"
A poem	"
A description of my family.	"

T. A weekly action plan for improving spelling

Name: ....   Date: ....

Writing needs: ....

....

....

(Give examples of the type of writing which you need to do or would like to do).

....

....

....

Spellings to be learned this week: ....

....

....

Spelling pattern to look for this week: ....

....

....

The method of learning spelling to be practised this week: ....

....

....

Writing planned for this week

Homework this week: ....

....

....

The method of assessing how much I learned: ....

....

....

Spellings learned	Spellings with the same pattern	Record of homework	Words which came up during the week

Assessment: ....
....
....

Learning shown by: ....
....
....

Difficulties encountered: ....
....
....

Next I would like to: ....
....
....

- Assessment criteria

  You'll need to agree with the student:

  – what evidence will be used to demonstrate that they have achieved their objectives

  – the date when progress will next be formally reviewed

  – the frequency of the intended class contact

  – the likely pattern of home study.

U. Practise, practise, practise

Student's progress will depend very largely on the amount of writing which they do. But students who have identified themselves as having a problem with spelling are often reluctant to write. You may therefore need to provide motivation for writing and lots of different reasons for students to put pen to paper. Some ideas are suggested below.

The most important writing tasks are the ones which the student identifies at the outset, but in many cases you will want to encourage students to extend their writing roles.

Workbased writing

A student who is applying for jobs could produce a good CV in class and perhaps a reduced version of it that could be used for form filling. One of these might be produced in a format which made it portable and particularly useful for ready reference. This could be laminated if it was likely to be regularly referred to or it could be put into a plastic wallet. A student who has to write out orders at work can keep a list of items which they know might need to be written down.

You may find it helpful to keep available examples of the things which students need to write in a work situation.

Keep examples of forms to be filled in, particularly those from newspapers and magazines where the content may match the interests of your student. For students who are actually looking for work, you will keep a selection of appropriate application forms.

Course work

Encourage students whose studies demand note-taking for course purposes to feel that notes for their own reference may not need to be perfectly spelt. However such notes provide a good opportunity to build up good spelling habits. This is particularly so with regard to technical terms and common words which they will also use in more extended pieces of writing.

Notes

Do encourage students to write notes as often as possible. Write some yourself, particularly ones which demand a written response. Also encourage your student to write notes to other students, to people at home and to anyone else you can think of. Students who write infrequently can make a start with short and simple notes addressed to someone with whom they feel comfortable to communicate in writing. As they build up skills and confidence these short notes can be extended and addressed to a widening and more impersonal audience.

Letter writing

All students should be encouraged to become letter writers as this provides the good purposeful activity for frequent practice. If they claim to have no friends or relatives to whom they can write perhaps they can write to newspapers or magazines or you may be able to make contact with a pen-friend scheme.

Writing in class

Some students need such prompts, even before they put pen to paper so you may collect or devise questionnaires which students can complete.

You will certainly need worksheets for students to use. The base where you work will probably have some and you may want to make some of your own to meet specific needs.

Writing at home

There are lots of games which involve writing. You could acquire some for your student to use if they are acceptable.

A student who is nervous about writing cheques could keep words for numbers written in the back of the cheque book. A student who writes letters can have a pro forma letter ready to refer to.

Another very useful activity for writing practice is diary writing. Once again the reluctant writer may start off with terse and simple summaries of their days. But if they will share what they have written, by gentle prompting and questioning you can encourage them to explain **why** and **how** they did things, what happened **next** and how they **felt** about it.

V. How do you spell this?

When a student asks for a correct spelling your response should depend upon the situation:

. . . If a student is in the middle of writing something they can be encouraged to disregard spelling and concentrate on meaning. Spelling is best dealt with at the proof reading stage, but lots of students nevertheless will ask for spellings in mid-flow of writing.

The best response is to provide the correct written form of the word in whatever way will most facilitate the student continuing with the current piece of writing away. That often means on a slip of paper that the student can then place in a convenient position to refer to (**but never copy from**). If the correct spelling of the word might be useful to any other student present you might write it on the black or whiteboard or on an OHP.

Do not say the letters of a spelling for the student to write. Spellings given **verbally** are difficult to catch correctly and result in errors. Also, saying a spelling does not help learning. By writing a spelling when it is requested you give visual reinforcement. By requesting the student to use Look, Cover, Write, Check (L,C,W,C) you encourage habits which help people to learn to spell.

The worst thing you can do is to interrupt the student's flow of thought by suggesting they use a dictionary or try to 'work it out' in some other way.

It is best to provide the correct form immediately without allowing it to interrupt the discussion or the teaching point.

. . . If the information is requested during a period of reflection, e.g. because the word has been used in conversation or a teaching context, it may be appropriate to suggest students try out the word for themselves then proof read to see if they think it 'looks right'.

In any event you will want to note down:

- words that your student had difficulty spelling

- the sort of difficulty

- if more than one student shared the problem.

You will want to use the information for diagnosis and planning.

The students will need to be forewarned that words or letter strings for attention will crop up from time to time. They will, therefore, need to equip themselves with the materials that will enable them to write down a single word for immediate reference or lists of words or letter strings that need their attention.

The best assessment is self-assessment and students need to become as independent as possible in checking their spellings. Effective proof reading involves close attentiveness allied with familiarity with reading and a good strategy for dealing with errors spotted.

Most students of spelling do not arrive with these skills, so they need to be developed as part of the learning programme.

This means that a tutor will have to be involved in marking and proof reading. But it is important to involve students at every stage in order to increase their independence.

W. The vocabulary of spelling

As with any other specialised skill there is a technical vocabulary for spelling. Whilst you don't want to put off students with unnecessarily complicated words neither do you want to patronise them by denying them access to a vocabulary which could help them. If they enjoy needlework or are keen swimmers they will no doubt know the specialised vocabulary for their interests.

There are some words with which you as a tutor will need to be very familiar and which students might find helpful in developing their skill:

- **Root**
- **Stem**
- **Prefix**
- **Suffix**
- **Syllable**

- **Vowel**
- **Consonant**
- **Verb**
- **Tense**
- **Morpheme.**

This list is not exhaustive. You will certainly need to be very familiar with all of these terms and be able to explain them clearly to your students.

Caution: the 'language' of spelling cannot be taught in one session. If you try to teach the terms without relating them to the particular aspects of spelling which you and your students are studying, you will forfeit your student's enthusiasm, and possibly their attendance!

X. Independent learning

To encourage students to become independent:

- DO NOT make decisions for them.
- Work to develop skills which will strengthen their independence. These skills are:
    - ☐ Asking Questions
    - ☐ Checking their own work

☐ Trying out difficult spellings

☐ Reflecting on what they do

☐ Thinking of ways to improve their learning

☐ Voicing opinions about what and how they learn.

Y. Recording spellings

Learning to spell successfully means learning as much as possible about the English language and being able to categorise words according to their spelling pattern. This means that your student needs to record words that they have learnt to spell. They should use their word lists as a reminder to write the words as frequently as possible and also to provide an insight into the structure of the language.

A simple way to record words initially is in a small notebook organised alphabetically.

You as the tutor will need to keep more comprehensive records of needs *(see Diagnosis on page 18)*.

From an initial list of individual words your student should progress to a bank of words organised according to visual patterns so that new words encountered can be placed in the appropriate section. It will clearly be helpful if there is a range of self access worksheets organised according to the same patterns.

But visual patterns are only one of many ways in which students need to categorise the spellings which they learn. They may wish to group words according to meaning or usage. Words for letter writing, words for cheques, words to do with their course, main interest or whatever categorisation most aids memory and retrieval.

Z. Testing

Students usually like to know how they are getting on. It is certainly helpful if they can clearly see the progress that they are making. You will obviously want to know where they have got to in the learning programme. It follows that the students' progress will need to be checked regularly. Sometimes this process is called **Testing** and students are very often much in favour of it.

There are lots of spelling tests available. **Don't use them**.

The only real test of spelling success is whether students are able to produce the writing they wish to do in an acceptable form. There is an important place for testing within the programme but it needs to address the specific learning needs which have been identified and to avoid distorting the teaching in any way.

What should be tested

If you test spelling more than other aspects of writing students will receive a clear message that spelling is more important than other things. So the testing of spelling needs to be put in the context of regular reviews of progress in all aspects of writing. The testing of spelling will need to encompass all the features which have been put into the learning programme for spelling development. These will probably include:

Proof-reading

As the student needs to develop proof reading skills for successful spelling, they should be encouraged to proof read everything they write and comment on the effectiveness of their writing. But you will need to test how accurate this proof reading is. If students are to improve their proof reading skills they will need feedback. You may limit this to some extent for students who miss a great deal in their proof-reading but have not yet developed sufficient confidence to have every error pointed out.

How

If you record the relative accuracy of your students proof reading you can compare progress over time. But, with increasing confidence, students may become more ambitious in their writing and therefore be increasing the difficulty of the task. This will invalidate comparisons but not the scrutiny of the effectiveness of proof reading. It remains important for the student to proof read accurately at the level at which they are writing.

Accuracy can be improved by setting the student a target number of errors to find. Never ask for more than about five even if there are more unspotted errors in a particular piece of the student's writing.

Testing Letter Strings

Improving spelling means becoming familiar with the common letter strings in English. As part of your assessment procedures you will be identifying the letter strings which are causing most confusion. For learning and testing purposes you will need to limit the number of letter strings tackled at any one time. It can often be best to stick to just one as working on it will be likely to introduce more letter strings which need attention.

How

As far as possible test the letter strings within a whole word. Choose letter strings which the student has been learning, for example – **tion**.

But don't choose too many words which are likely to bring in a whole range of additional letter strings to be learned.

Choose words which your student is most likely to use or need or be familiar with.

Remember you are testing **-tion**, not at this stage the other letter strings contained in the words. The student needs to understand this distinction so that they can record specific learning achieved.

- **Station**
- **Ration**
- **Emotion**
- **Notion**
- **Caution**
- **Constipation**

- **Corruption**
- **Direction**
- **Generation**
- **Motion**
- **Potion**
- **Dictation**

- **Relation**
- **Nation**
- **Distinction**
- **Transportation**
- etc.

Example of students' record of progress on learning letter strings.

'I can write it accurately.'

'I can write it accurately when it is part of a larger word.'

'I have recorded the letter string.'

'I have identified other words with the same letter string.'

'I have found out how this letter string came into the English language.'

Testing words

If you have only one student you can certainly test the words which have been identified for learning within a specific time scale. This may form a regular part of your teaching programme. Knowing that words will be tested encourages students to work between contact times.

Test:

- the words which the student has selected to learn
- words which contain the same letter string and which may be needed by the student
- words which demonstrate a rule which students have discovered for themselves
- words in context relevant to the student.

The student needs to know that having spelt the words correctly in a test is only part of the testing procedure. Frequent practice of the word will be necessary using self-checking to ensure that the practice is continuing to achieve the desired results. You will need to test again after a longer gap.

How

1.

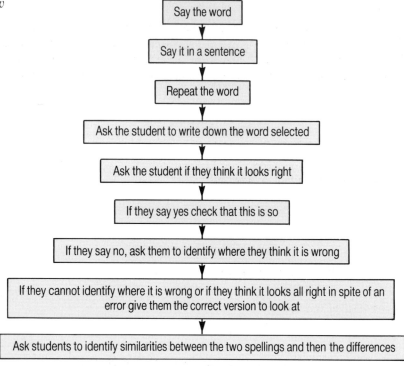

Say the word

Say it in a sentence

Repeat the word

Ask the student to write down the word selected

Ask the student if they think it looks right

If they say yes check that this is so

If they say no, ask them to identify where they think it is wrong

If they cannot identify where it is wrong or if they think it looks all right in spite of an error give them the correct version to look at

Ask students to identify similarities between the two spellings and then the differences

2. Give the student sentences which contain the words but leave gaps for the words to be tested.

3. Give the students definitions of the words to be tested.

It is essential that **wherever** possible students spot errors for themselves and make attempts to put them right.

Example of record of student progress.

'I can write the word correctly if I stop to think about it.'

'I can write the word correctly without thinking about it.'

'I can write the word correctly in one continuous flow.'

'I can write the word correctly as part of a sentence.'

'I regularly write the word correctly even though it is: a week/a month/a year/since I first learned to spell it.'

34

Strategies

Your student will need to use a range of strategies for learning spellings. You will want to check that they do in fact develop some new strategies and do not just rely on ones which they came with and which may have failed them in the past. You will also want to know which strategies work best for the student as this may guide your planning for teaching new strategies.

How

You will have to ask your student which methods they are using. Try to observe the strategy in action if this is possible. Test the results so you can discuss with your student the best ways for them to learn.

Dictation

You may wish to use **dictation** as a testing device.

Try to use something written by a student if possible.

In any event you will want to be sure that the language and vocabulary are those which would be used by the student.

How

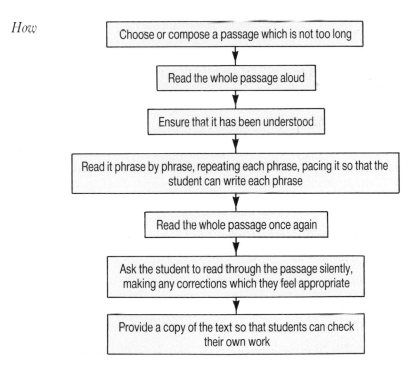

Choose or compose a passage which is not too long

Read the whole passage aloud

Ensure that it has been understood

Read it phrase by phrase, repeating each phrase, pacing it so that the student can write each phrase

Read the whole passage once again

Ask the student to read through the passage silently, making any corrections which they feel appropriate

Provide a copy of the text so that students can check their own work

Testing rules

You will not be teaching by **rules** but you will encourage your student to notice or discover rules. This means that you will structure learning material so that students notice regularities such as:

Dictate	Dictation
Relate	Relation
Constipate	Constipation
Motivate	Motivation
Generate	Generation.

You may then test this learning by producing a list of words which demonstrate a particular regularity and by asking the student to spell them or by providing a list of verbs and asking students to provide the matching list of nouns etc.

The pattern of testing

You will need to test regularly. But a pattern of testing where you check on words learned each week should only be part of the picture. The student needs to spell correctly in writing done outside of class.

Encourage students to bring in such samples of writing as they will help you to see how they are getting on. But you may not be able to do all the necessary testing with pieces of writing done in this way.

Other forms of testing are simulations. For greatest validity you will need to create conditions which are, as far as possible, like the real thing.

That means encouraging the student to write pieces in class which may subsequently be used outside of class.

Each time students use you, other class members or class materials as a resource the outcomes will be affected. You will want them to move towards independence in the activity. You cannot assume that they will make the jump from successful completion of class tests to success in independent writing tasks performed **out** of class.

Validity of testing processes

You need to be aware that the activities which are devised for testing spelling may be more or less predictive of accurate spelling in a real context depending on how contrived they are.

The list of words tested after one week tells you that the student can spell the words selected with some preparation, with the aural prompt and with the stimulus of wanting to please teacher after a gap of one week from last being taught.

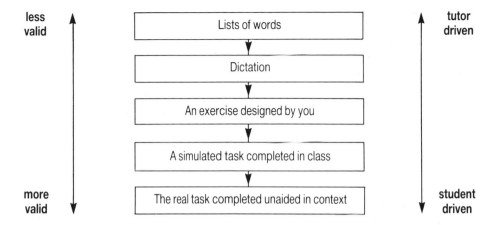

Regular writing which students successfully proof read and use for real purposes is a much more valid form of testing.

2 | Helping your Student to Spell

Teaching and learning spelling

It is doubtful whether you can teach someone to spell; but certain that you can show someone how to learn to spell. There is no one system which can guarantee to improve a person's spelling because each of us has a unique set of learning styles, and we tend to use different spelling strategies depending upon the word in question. This section of the book describes and illustrates a variety of techniques you may draw on with your student, and which they can try themselves. They may not like some of them, or you might not like them, in which case ignore them. It doesn't really matter how they learn to spell as long as they are eventually able to recall the spellings and reproduce in writing the words they want to use. If they become a really 'good' speller, they will eventually do this automatically.

Don't ask a student to learn a word without:

- **Showing them a way of doing so**

- **Explaining why the word is spelt that way**

- **Helping them to identify other words with the same pattern**.

You will find lots of examples of different methods of learning to spell. Here some of the most popular will be described. If a method works for your student it's worth using – if it doesn't work then no matter how much it has been recommended by someone else, there is no point in using it. But remain aware of it. It may be useful for a different student.

Always remember that spelling is a **visuo-motor** skill. This means that the **visual** and **physical** aspects of spelling cannot be ignored. They are the most crucial. Other approaches used can only augment and support them. If students are to make progress in spelling they must **see** and **feel** the patterns of **English**, only then will they be able to reproduce them reliably.

Also remember that your student will learn best if involved in a **planned** programme. Tackling words on a one-off basis as they crop up reinforces the student's view of spelling as a whimsical system. If they are to see logic and purpose in it, that logic and purpose will need to come initially from **you**.

Although you should use the methods which work for your students there are some clear **do's** and **don't** in relation to spelling.

Do's

- Encourage students to group words together according to how they **look** rather than how they sound.

- Encourage students to keep a word book where words are grouped in this way.

- Encourage students to write whole words in one movement if possible rather than lots of letters.

- Concentrate on **writing**. Spelling is only a small part of this and should be seen as a tool to facilitate the students' writing.

- Encourage prediction and guessing of possible spellings.

- Encourage students to write frequently – every day is good, several times a day much more likely to lead to success; once a week certainly isn't enough.

- Help students to build up the skills which will lead to independence; reading, visualisation, proof reading, handwriting or keyboarding, composing, drafting, editing.

- Analyse students' writing regularly. Record and build on strengths as well as using weaknesses as a starting point.

- Use the analysis to devise a coherent programme of which spelling will usually be a small part.

- Provide self access materials.

- Encourage interest and pleasure in the English language.

- Keep looking out for new ways in which your students can learn to remember spellings.

But don't

- Don't ever encourage your student to copy words – spelling means being able to write the word down correctly when it is **not** in front of you.

A. The visual approach

For most human beings vision is the preferred sense. Spelling is a visual skill. Many students find visual approaches to learning to spell particularly helpful.

Students need to **notice** the features of words if they are to spell them correctly. You will therefore need to find lots of ways to generate and focus such attentive behaviour. Here are some ways you might do it:

1. Look, See, Cover, Imagine, Write, Check, Practise

Look

The student needs to start from a good copy of the word. This can be presented on paper, in the student's notebook, on a white or blackboard, on an OHP or on a strip of card – a flash card.

The student needs to be able to read this word before it's worth proceeding. The word should be written in unjoined lower case letters with capital initials where appropriate. This provides a word shape which helps students to visualise the word.

See

The next stage is to **notice**. It's a special kind of looking with a determined intention to **remember**. If, as is likely, the student has already had trouble spelling this word it will be apparent where attention needs to be focused.

The student should be encouraged to look for as short a time as possible before they feel confident that they will be able to remember it. They should also say the word, preferably aloud.

Imagine

Now the word must be covered up. It is important that the word can be 'seen' when it is not there. The student needs to visualise the word. This will be helped if the student once again says the word aloud.

Write

Now the student writes the word, preferably in one flowing movement.

Check

The student should now proof read the word which they have written to see if they think it looks right.

The experienced student will be able to deal with this proof reading independently but for less experienced students it is important to check that they are right. If they have written the word correctly, they will need to follow the activity up with some regular practice at writing and using the word as much as possible.

If they have spelt the word wrongly but **thought** it was right they need to do some work on **proof reading** as well as activities to improve their **attentiveness** and **recollection**.

If they have spelt the word wrongly and have spotted their mistake they will need to identify the part of the word that they've got wrong.

They should then start the process again, focusing particular attention on the part of the word where they made an error.

In every case they should write down the whole word. It is not a good idea to correct bits of a word. The actual writing of the word helps in remembering it, particularly if the writing is accompanied by the student saying the word aloud.

The student who has consistent problems with this approach may need much more help in visualising words:

- It is easier to start with small words.

- Say the word.

- Exaggerate parts of the sounds.

- Refer to the physical features of the words.

- Draw a box round the word to become familiar with its shape, *(see Marjorie on page 40)*.

- Encourage students to 'see' the word in a decorative or ridiculous context.

2. Looking attentively at words

To do this **students** need to see how words are made up of separate meaning units like building bricks which can be put in different positions to produce lots of different results.

Examples:

con	**struct**	**ure**
re	**flu**	**tion**
ob		**ence**
in		
de		

This really can't be achieved fully in occasional teaching time. Looking for such units needs to become a habit. Encourage your students to identify some, perhaps starting with their own name or address or interests. It really helps if students can spot semantically significant units.

In every case, the student, having identified a word with the letter string should:

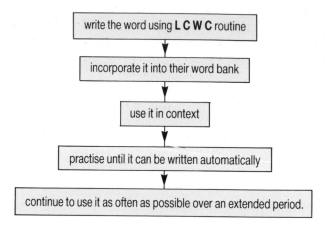

write the word using **L C W C** routine

↓

incorporate it into their word bank

↓

use it in context

↓

practise until it can be written automatically

↓

continue to use it as often as possible over an extended period.

One activity would be:

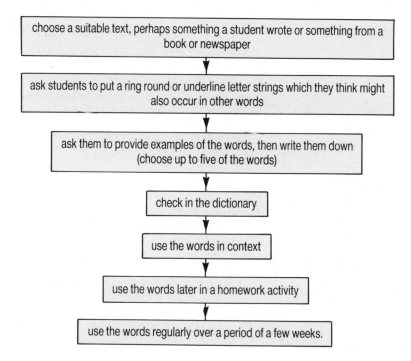

choose a suitable text, perhaps something a student wrote or something from a book or newspaper

↓

ask students to put a ring round or underline letter strings which they think might also occur in other words

↓

ask them to provide examples of the words, then write them down (choose up to five of the words)

↓

check in the dictionary

↓

use the words in context

↓

use the words later in a homework activity

↓

use the words regularly over a period of a few weeks.

3. Flash cards

These are strips of card on which are written words which the student might need to learn to spell. It's particularly important to have them available for words which don't have predictable auditory patterns and will therefore be best learnt by a visual approach. But the visual approach is in any case important for all students and therefore flash cards are valuable teaching aids.

The size of the card will depend upon the use to which you intend to put it. If it is for a group of students it will need to be larger than for an individual.

The quality will probably depend on the anticipated frequency of use. If it's just a one-off you won't need to print and laminate it but if you think it will be used repeatedly or with several students you might think that it's worth more trouble. Remember to use lower case writing.

Additional purposes
Flash cards have the virtue of providing an uncluttered visual image which is ideal for stimulating **visualisation** and **memory**.

4. Games

Word squares are useful ways to encourage students to 'find' a particular letter string. You could make some specially or get students to do so. If you teach more than one student you could encourage them to make squares for each other on a friendly/

A word search puzzle on 'Driving' (25 words to find)

```
S   C H O K E H   T H P
A R A D I A T O R Y A E
F F R A I N G L   R T T
E A T N B T   E   E G R
T R A G U I C E A   L O
Y O R E S F M E N R O L
T H I R D R     B   V R
  A C O G E N G I N E U
M I P O W E R A K   S S
I N H O G Z   T E I N T
N F A S T E M U S C L E
I N S U R A N C E O I L
```

Suggestions for word-search puzzle topics:

– The End of the World!

– Animals

– Television

– Spelling

– Countries

– Politics

– Gardening

– Looking for Work

– Families

from 'The Spelling Pack', ALBSU

competitive basis. Ensure words are only read left to right and top to bottom; this provides correct sequencing of letter patterns which reinforce visualisation strategies.

Additional purpose

The word square should always be accompanied by a list of the words contained so that the student is looking for specific words. This encourages the brain to form a visual image of the word even before it is actually spotted by the eye. This type of stimulation of visualisation is good training for spellers.

Word jigsaws

Provide bits of words which can go together in different combinations:

be	day
lit	fore
mon	ter
cen	age
post	tury
to	sert
in	gether
im	form
trans	port
re	do

when students have made the connections they should write each word in full and then write it in an appropriate context.

Additional purpose

Putting together parts of words like this produces a closure of the type used in **cloze** exercises. It encourages the brain to complete a pattern. It also stimulates **visualisation**.

Word columns

You can construct columns of words which share a common letter string. You could also get your student to do this independently or to work in a group to produce a word column.

Additional purpose

The grouping of words together in an ordered way such as a column is very helpful as an aid to memory. It also provides a mechanism for categorising according to the visual features of the word.

44

SPELLING

The letter string: **dec**
as in <u>dec</u>ide

<u>dec</u>ent   <u>dec</u>imal

<u>dec</u>ided   <u>dec</u>ision

<u>dec</u>eit   <u>dec</u>lare

fit the letters into the gaps below:

.... ide   .... ision   .... ent

.... imal   .... lare   .... ided

Now fit the words into the grid below:

Now choose 2
of the words and
write them into
2 sentences.

5. Words within words

Once students have got the message that words are composed of meaning units, they need to be on the look-out for such units all the time. You will point them out where appropriate but also encourage them to do so out of class contact time, e.g. **Man**chest**er**.

e.g. **Spot the word**

This can be done by a group of students or by individuals. For students who don't find it immediately easy you might prepare a text which is particularly rich in words which contain smaller words. It can also be helpful to provide cards or a sheet of paper with the small words on.

It is a good idea if the words can be highlighted or underlined in the text. They should be written down using the LCWC procedure.

The student needs to understand that the more frequently a string of letters is written the more permanently they become embedded in the memory. It is also important for the student to know that a very large proportion of long words will have smaller words within them. Practising the smaller words therefore contributes in a very real sense to being able to spell longer words; the skill being not only in knowing the letter strings but in the body's memory of writing them.

The spot the word activity provides a useful extension to work outside the classroom. The student can be encouraged to look out for examples during the week. If they write them down whenever it is convenient to do so, their spelling will improve. The aim with any spelling is to be able to write it automatically without thinking of its component parts.

The spot the word routine can be used to fit in with each new spelling pattern which is being learned. The student should be praised for bringing in examples of words that have been spotted and those words should be used if possible during contact time, for instance by:

- being shown to another student

- by asking the student to remember in what context they were seen

- putting the words into bigger ones

- breaking the words down into small ones

- thinking of other words with similar patterns

- using the words in context

- putting them in a word bank

- incorporating them into a writing task

- incorporating them into a dictation.

Errors

If the student brings in words which are incorrectly spelt you'll need to try to trace back whether your student wrongly recognised the pattern or wrote down the pattern incorrectly.

If the student is 'spotting' the letter string incorrectly you'll need to do more work on **visual discrimination**, **memorising** and **visualisation**. If students write words down incorrectly they probably need more practice at writing short familiar words. In either case it would seem clear that they need **proof reading** practice.

6. Discrimination

You can provide words with similar patterns

- spot the difference
- explain the difference
- mark the difference
- use in appropriate contexts.

Additional purpose
Differences in spelling of words which sound the same or are in other ways similar are not arbitrary. Often there are good reasons for the differences. Examining words and tracing their development is beneficial to the speller. Curiosity about words usually leads to improvements in spelling.

Visual Discrimination

SAMPLE WORKSHEET

Look at the pairs of words in the list below.

How are the words in each pair different?

Mark the parts of the words which are different in each pair.

Explain the difference in meaning to a partner or your tutor.

Now use the words in sentences which show the differences.

their	there	meet	meat
wear	where	feet	feat
hear	here	no	know
bare	bear	Peter	peter
practice	practise	quite	quiet
stationery	stationary	rows	rose
course	coarse	nose	knows
flower	flour	pleas	please
grown	groan	teas	tease
hole	whole	watt	what

NB: This should not be used with students who constantly confuse such words as this is likely to compound it. You should limit the number of words included to match the student's learning capacity.

B. Developing skills of visualisation

It is very important that students form a visual image of words which they want to be able to spell.

You can help them to do this:

1. Train students in Look – Cover – Write – Check

(See Visual Methods 1)

BUT it is important that they **look** for as short a time as possible. They probably will not be able to visualise the word after only a brief look. This means they need to pay more **attention** to the make up of the word **not** that they need to look at it for a longer period.

The noticing part is where knowledge and experience come in and where your enthusiasm for the language will help.

The student needs to **see** the significant parts of the word (that is significant for the student, probably the letter strings which they spell incorrectly). These are readily identified by looking at the student's written version of the word. It is important to help the student to identify the parts which have been written correctly (if there are any). Then the student needs to get a visual fix on the difficult bits. Use any knowledge or technique that helps.

The student will need to write or trace the difficult letter strings until they can do it with their eyes shut. Then they need to go through the same activity with the whole word. It is important that this activity is followed up by writing **from memory** the word into the word book or word bank. It is crucial that they see the word alongside others which share the same letter string. They should then write those words, first as individual words and then in context. This is a place where dictation is very useful to ensure that the student has an opportunity and a reason to write words containing the letter string in a context where there is no opportunity for copying. The more students find **visualising** difficult the more they need a **multi-sensory** approach which will reinforce the impression of the word and fix it in the mind so it can be visualised.

2. Games

Crosswords

There are plenty of books of crosswords available. Doing any crossword will help spelling provided that the student **can** complete them and **enjoys** doing them. It is also a beneficial activity for students to construct their own or to work in pairs and groups to construct them. This has the virtue of ensuring that the words used are ones which the student knows and uses. The procedure can further be refined to include words containing particular strings. *(see Example No.3)*.

CH and SH words

batch	chart	itch	dash	shingle	sharp
snatch	chat	machine	sash	brush	flash
church	watch	march	shirt	finish	ash
lurch	scratch	watch	splash	fashion	bush
chime	birch	ache	fishing	wash	
match					

ACROSS

1. Opposite to start. (6)
3. A short conversation. (4)
6. Month after February. (5)
7. Pointed (5)
12. What you do with soap and water. (4)
13. It goes with trousers. (5)
15. Sewing . . . (7)
16. A type of tree. (3)
17. Small stones on a beach. (7)

DOWN

1. . . . in the pan. (5)
2. To get rid of an itch. (7)
4. A kind of pain. (4)
5. A place to pray. (6)
8. You'll need a rod and some bait doing this. (7)
9. The sound of a door bell. (5)
10. A little stick that has a flame. (5)
11. Just scratch this. (4)
14. To sprint in short bursts. (4)

Additional purpose

Successful completion of crosswords requires knowledge of serial probability and also encourages closure. It calls for recall of whole words through visual, linguistic and semantic cues. Such stimulation of **recall** is of great benefit to the speller.

Hangman

Hangman is a good game for focusing attention on specific bits of a word. It also has the virtue of being very easy to set up, using paper & pencil or blackboard/whiteboard. Once again students can prepare words for one another using particular letter strings.

Additional purpose

Successful completion of Hangman depends upon knowledge of serial probability. This knowledge is one of the main features which distinguish good spellers from less successful ones.

3. Cloze

You are no doubt familiar with the use of cloze procedure for reading. You can also use the brain's desire to complete patterns for spelling purposes. Once the difficult part of a word has been identified **write** the word, whiting out the difficult bit, e.g.

schooner ooner

Ask the student to look at the whole word briefly but with the intention to remember. Then show the word with the gap. Ask the student if they can 'picture' what should be written in the gap. If they can't do this show them the complete word once again, asking them to focus on the difficult bit.

Repeat the process until the student can write the whole word correctly. Once again students who have difficulty with this need a **multi-sensory** approach, tracing and writing first the parts which they have found difficult, then the whole word whilst saying it, aloud is best. Then they **see**, **feel** and **hear** at the same time.

You can provide, or encourage students to provide a word with letters missing thus focusing attention on a particular bit of a word. Alternatively you can provide a whole passage which includes selected words with gaps, or you can provide a table of words with gaps for completion. An easy and simple method for creating gaps in existing material is to use 'Snopake' or some other similar print whitener which has the virtues of creating gaps instantly, of being user friendly and of providing a base for inserting the required letters.

When I went to Grey Friars

My first day at Grey Friars was the most frightening day of my life. It was the hardest thing I have ever done. I went round and round the car park before I went into the school but when I did it was the best thing I have ever done in my life. I have met some lovely people at Grey Friars, they are the most dedicated people I have ever met.

The first day I came to Grey Friars I was a non reader but now I can read and write

Tony Guest

Additional purpose

For successful spelling the brain must 'see' words in their complete form. This is **visualisation**; it is a skill which is necessary for spelling and which can be trained. **Cloze** exercises are a good way of training students in visualisation.

C. The auditory approach

Vision is the preferred sense for most people. Unless you are working with visually impaired students (in which case you will need more specialised guidance) it is *only* through **visual** familiarity with language that your student can learn about the probable spelling of words. Spelling is, afterall, about visual sequences of letters. However many students rely on auditory methods and need to harness their auditory sense to reinforce learning through other modes. Saying words, lingering over letters and exaggerating distinctions can all help but it is crucially important that where bits of words are used as clues they are always seen as part of the whole word. It is learning to visualise the whole word which improves spelling.

Auditory approaches should only be used as an aid to visualisation. Some which might be helpful are described here.

1. Sound to letter correspondence

Although the sound to letter correspondence in English is not exact much English does in fact fit into clear patterns of correspondence. Often the spelling does reflect pronunciation and saying a word can give clues or even very clear indications of likely spelling.

You can enable students to see for instance that in one syllabled words a final "k" sound is almost always produced by "**ck**" as in thi**ck**, tri**ck**, si**ck**, bri**ck**, li**ck**.

2. Doubling

A single consonant in the middle of a word normally follows a long vowel:

ha*ting*	bi*ting*	ho*ping*
ma*ting*	wri*ting*	ro*ping*
ra*ting*	si*ting*	co*ping*

A double consonant in the middle of a word normally follows a short vowel:

ma*tting*	ne*tting*	si*tting*	po*tting*	cu*tting*
ba*tting*	pe*tting*	pi*tting*	bo*ttle*	bu*tton*
pa*tting*	ge*tting*	hi*tting*	thro*ttle*	mu*tton*

This is a useful regularity for spellers to be aware of and gives them clues about the spelling of words such as:

collapse	*million*
colon	*voting*
shallow	

but only if they understand the concept of long and short vowels. It follows that it is important that these concepts are taught to students who have not already developed them and who wish to use an auditory approach.

3. Pronunciation

Silent letters

This can be helpful to remind students of "silent letters". Sounding out words like:

k̲not   _k̲now_   _k̲nife_   _g̲naw_   _g̲nome_   _g̲nash_

may be of benefit though the learning can also be tackled through visual approaches. Students may also like to know of the history of the words which provide reasons for some apparant anomalies.

Unpronounced letters and syllables
Sounding out the whole word can enable students to remember the spellings.

| FEB **R**UARY | WED NES DAY | PARL I A MENT | GOV ER**N** MENT |

4. Groups of words

For less confident spellers it can be helpful to teach words in groups which share a common visual pattern and share a sound pattern.

share	_fear_	_boat_
pare	_hear_	_coat_
hare	_gear_	_gloat_
bare	_dear_	_stoat_
care	_near_	_float_
dare	_rear_	_moat_

If you adopt this approach you should avoid introducing the homophonic words which have different spellings. This approach lends itself to using **rhymes** and **jingles** which some students find helpful and some do not.

N.B. By choosing letter strings which sound the same you give students the message that, for instance, '**EAR**', always says 'ear', this doesn't equip them for words which don't follow this auditory pattern, e.g. wear, tear.

D. Kinaesthetic approaches

Spelling is primarily a **visuo-motor** skill. This means that it relies on knowledge of the **look** of words but also on the **feel** of writing them. It is the repeated writing of words which fixes the spelling in the memory just as much as looking at them. C is often followed by K. Our hand 'knows' this. C is rarely followed by D so it's actually harder to write down. Finger tracing is sometimes advocated, though for adults actual writing is probably more acceptable. Its effectiveness is less because of the reduced kinaesthetic feedback caused by the intervention of the writing implements. But this disadvantage is soon wiped out with sufficient practice in writing particular words. Even using a word processor provides kinaesthetic feedback which is useful to the speller and which can trigger the correct spelling of words.

This physical component of spelling needs to be harnessed for success. It is the reason why the reluctant writer will have great difficulty in improving spelling and why you need to motivate and stimulate writing as much as possible.

Handwriting

It is well established that legible and fluent handwriting strongly assists spelling. It follows that students who write haltingly and who are not consistent and logical in letter formation may benefit from improving their handwriting. If they show an interest in improving handwriting it is useful to incorporate handwriting into the overall programme. But many students will not acknowledge any difficulty with handwriting and may be fluent writers though producing poorly formed and unformed letters. It would not be appropriate for you to shake the confidence of such students though you might gradually encourage them to consider spelling in relation to handwriting. One way is to get them to read their own handwriting aloud.

For those who do want to improve, spelling offers ideal patterns to practise. It is important that such students are fully aware of how strongly the skills of spelling and handwriting reinforce each other.

The writing practice can be linked to any of the other approaches suggested here (e.g. *Words within words*).

E. Logical

There are people who claim that the English spelling system is illogical. There is plenty of evidence to refute them. You need to be an advocate of the logical aspects of English if you are not to de-motivate students.

You must help them to see the logic of the language. That means ensuring that they understand something about its history and that each part of the picture which is presented relates to the rest. It also means encouraging students to use all parts of their brains, particularly the parts which work best for them.

The logic of English spelling:

- derives in part from a sound to letter correspondence which, though imperfect, can be harnessed to enable students to categorise spellings and remember them. This will be aided by systematic **recording** and the development of **information retrieval skills**.

- relates to the relationship between reading and spelling, the specific spelling often providing information about meaning which enables the reader to be more efficient.

- is also based on the history of the language which not only provides the reasons for differences in spelling but also the way to understand those differences and use them as aids to remembering spellings.

- is mainly related to the **meanings** of words and syllables. Encouraging students to look at these in a logical way will assist them to develop a coherent and positive view of the language.

To take this logical approach you will need to sieze every opportunity which presents itself. Luckily such opportunities frequently arise.

1. Syllables

For improving spelling it is not a good idea to laboriously sound out spellings, breaking them down into syllables as an auditory exercise. The research that has been done on spelling suggests that such reliance on the sound of words is counter-productive as it is the **visual** features of the word which are significant for spelling. However **visualisation** requires attention to the detail of words and methods which help visualisation should be used. Looking at how words are made up is very important. It will inevitably involve some examination of grammar, pronunciation and the history of the language. It will also clearly mean a close examination of the make-up of words and therefore an understanding of **syllables**. But it is syllables that carry meaning that can best be used to focus the *visual* attention of the student.

dis   en   chant   ed

Each bit of the word warrants investigation and explanation. And each bit in its turn, successfully spelled, will contribute to the writing and spelling of other words.

Difficulty with syllables arises with double letters and there is often unresolved confusion about what constitutes a syllable, for instance:

be   gin   ning
be   ginn   ing

2. Meaningful letter strings

Morphemes

A morpheme is the smallest unit of meaning in a word.

dis   un   sci   ness

These are all examples of morphemes. It is important that your student becomes used to dealing in this currency. The student needs to be able to look at a word and pick out the different morphemes which make up the total meaning of the word. This is not the same as breaking words into syllables – breaking words into syllables is not likely to be helpful to your student, looking for morphemic units is. The student should be focussing their visual attention on the word, not trying to sound it out. Sounding it out is detrimental to good spelling as it is not meaningful. You should discourage students from doing it.

An examination of morphemes will be enhanced if it is done in conjunction with an exploration of their grammatical role. Many morphemes are used as **prefixes** and **suffixes**. You will be better able to help students develop their spelling skills if you are able to discuss these matters using the correct technical terms.

3. Root words

Students are often put off simply by the length of a word and feel that they will never be able to spell words containing more than a few letters. They need to understand and to **see** that often the longest words are potentially the easiest to learn. They need to understand that each part of the word carries meaning. In each word there is a core element of meaning which is the root of the word. For many small words this will constitute the word's entirety e.g. egg. But many words have additional components which carry meaning. In English these are added to the beginning or ending of the root word e.g. 's' as in 'eggs' to signify plurality.

4. Prefixes

Morphemes which are added at the beginning of words are called **Prefixes**. You can use the word to illustrate the meaning for students.

pre	**fix**	**es**
in front of	attached	more than one

You can encourage students to find and use lots of other examples:

trans	**pose**
change	position

	mis	trust	
		fortune	inform
		take	appropriate
		cast	shapen

Remember to let your students know the good news about prefixes. They do not alter the spelling of the root word. This is a rule which might well be useful to them. *(see Example Nos. 4 and 5.)*

PREFIXES

1. Write the opposites of the words by changing the letters that have been underlined.

1.	include	6.	overwork
2.	encourage	7.	exhale
3.	deflate	8.	demote
4.	increase	9.	decrease
5.	import	10.	ascend

1. Write the opposites of these words, using a prefix each time. Choose prefixes from this list below. You can use some of them more than once.

'dis', 'im', 'in', 'mis', 'non', 'un'.

1.	understanding	6.	certainty
2.	happiness	7.	agreement
3.	patience	8.	attention
4.	appearance	9.	sense
5.	gratitude	10.	advantage

3. Now use each prefix twice:

'dis', 'im', 'in', 'ir', 'un'.

1.	polite	5.	avoidable	9.	pure
2.	honest	6.	replaceable	10.	credible
3.	visible	7.	courteous		
4.	relevant	8.	believable		

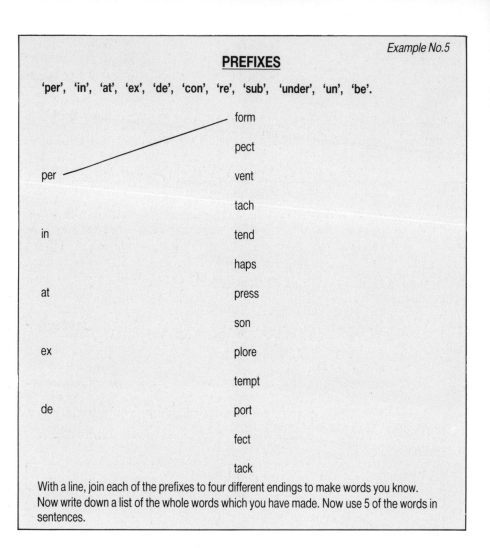

PREFIXES

'per', 'in', 'at', 'ex', 'de', 'con', 're', 'sub', 'under', 'un', 'be'.

	form
	pect
per	vent
	tach
in	tend
	haps
at	press
	son
ex	plore
	tempt
de	port
	fect
	tack

With a line, join each of the prefixes to four different endings to make words you know.
Now write down a list of the whole words which you have made. Now use 5 of the words in
sentences.

5. Suffixes

You can illustrate the role of suffixes in different ways. Here are two which would suit
students at different levels of competence and confidence;

1. Introduce each suffix pattern separately, starting off with those which don't alter
the spelling of the original word. Discuss how the meaning of the words listed is
modified by the addition of –**ness**. Then discuss the fact that the spelling of each word
is not changed by the addition of –**ness**:

Fitness	paleness	boldness
badness	sameness	hardness
(end in one consonant)	(end in silent 'e')	(end in two consonants)

You can then go on to study words which **do** change e.g. those which **double** their final letter before a suffix starting with a vowel:

fitting,   tapped,   spinner,   reddest.

Try to find as many examples as possible of the patterns. Use words from the student's own writing if you can. You can then decide whether it would be a good idea for your student to generate a rule from the patterns. Then provide lots of ideas and opportunities for the student to use each pattern as much as possible in interesting and relevant writing activity *(see Example Nos. 6 and 7)*.

COMMON SUFFIXES

Example No.6

Which suffixes can be used?

	s	ed	al	ing
station				
nation				
ration				
education				
action				
question				
addition				
portion				

Tick the boxes if you think the suffix can be used with the word.

Write out the complete words.

Write sentences containing the words.

SUFFIX: 'IVE'

Write the sentences, filling in the blanks with words chosen from this list:

corrosive   persuasive   impulsive

adhesive   oppressive   massive

evasive   abrasive   impressive

abusive

1. The speaker's manner was charming and ....

2. The .... heat made everyone feel tired.

3. When attacked, the aircraft took .... action.

4. His language was threatening and ....

5. An .... substance is sticky.

6. There was a .... landslide after the heavy rain.

7. The home team scored an .... win.

8. An .... act is one done without much thought.

9. An .... substance is used for scraping and rubbing.

10. Rust has a .... effect on metals.

2. For more advanced students you could demonstrate a range of suffix patterns by adding several to one root word:

fit,   fitter,   fits,   fitment,   fitting,   fitted.

This approach will demonstrate how the pattern is determined by the context and can lead to a more detailed exploration of the grammar connection. You can point out to the student that suffixes **never** change but they do sometimes change the words they are added to. It does help students to realise that suffixes carry an unchanging grammatical message with them, e.g.

s es	more than on a plural
ed	past tense
ing	present participle
able	capable of being
ly	indicates an adverb
cal	describes someone or something (it is usually an adjective)

6. Tense discrimination

Some students have difficulty with word endings, particularly those denoting tense. They may habitually use a present tense form, e.g.

- *collapse* for '*collapsed*'.

Sometimes they are not aware that they are thus using incorrect grammar. They can be helped by grammatical explanations and examples but also need some auditory discrimination practice. This can be turned into a game but can also be assisted by getting them to read their writing aloud. Where you do find any such lack of auditory discrimination of this kind it is important that you tackle it using auditory approaches. The student may well soon learn to discriminate **visually** in written exercises but if they are not noticing the difference in sound when they hear the word spoken they will continue to have difficulties in spelling words with similar endings. This is of particular importance in work with students for whom English is not a first language, and who have learnt some English 'by ear', without any background language or knowledge of grammar. If there is an acuity problem this will have to be tackled semantically. This can be done by encouraging students to ask themselves questions about **when** something happened in their writing and checking word endings on this basis.

7. Meanings

Get the student to think of words with particular meanings which contain the particular string: *(see Example No.8)*

All words start with **CON**. Write the whole word: *Example No.8*

A word which means a musical entertainment

Laura played the piano at the end of term con ....

A word which means a receptacle

He had put the flour in the con .... marked sugar.

A word which means easy or suitable

If you could come later it would be much more con ....

A word which means a pointed shape with a round base (like a wizard's hat)

She put a big scoop of ice cream into the con ....

A word which means to defeat an enemy

The Romans sent an army to Britain to con .... it.

A word which means a tree with cones!

She chopped down the con .... when it got too tall.

A word which means to keep or preserve

Robinson Crusoe tried to con .... his scarce resources.

A word which means having a different or opposite quality

He wore the red floral tie as a con .... to his sober suit.

A word which means a spoken exchange

Ann and James had a long con .... about Paul's school report.

A word which means a banged head

He was taken to hospital with con .... after the accident.

8. The history lesson

There are clear reasons for some common English spelling patterns. **Colchester** for instance shares a pattern with many other places in Britain i.e. *Ilchester, Manchester, Chichester*. Places with such names were Roman camps. The Latin word for them was

Castra. The English form of that is Chester (or in some place names *caster* e.g. Lancaster, or *cester*, e.g. Cirencester). So the place name is well established. If you have a student who travels around the country or lives near such a town or has to write down names or addresses, they may find such insights helpful and a stimulus to **looking** and **noticing**. Words which are not names can also be researched in this way.

Additional purposes
The historical approach encourages students to delve into the origins of words. This is an important activity for all who wish to improve their spelling. Besides providing stimulus and encouraging students to pose questions, word history is knowledge with status. Some students feel inadequate because they need help. Word history positively changes student's views of their learning, the language and themselves.

9. Rules

Encourage students to notice rules but do not present rules as a way of learning spellings. Encourage students to make up their own wording for describing regular patterns which they have noticed.

Any rules should:

- apply to a **large** number of words

- have **few** exceptions

- be **easy** to understand.

Some rules will already be familiar to students but should only be used if the above rules apply!

> e.g. **i** before **e** except after **c**

10. Imaginative approaches

Even when you use systematic approaches in helping students to spell and use all your knowledge of language to assist you, there will be some words which prove very difficult to fit into any of the prescribed patterns. That is when you need to encourage your students to use mental tricks to help them.

Mnemonics

A mnemonic is just a memory aid. The most effective will:

- generate a visual image, perhaps including a picture

- be made up by the student who needs them

(Example: **rhythm**

Rhythm **H**as **Y**our **T**wo **H**ips **M**oving)

It is only worth going to the trouble for words
which cannot be tackled in some simpler way
or which are likely to cause repeated
problems for the student.

Illustrated words

Visualisation is aided greatly if students **imagine** the word they want to learn. They
need to think about it and to 'see' it in front of them or in their heads. This process can
be aided by writing the word perhaps in a way which illustrates its meaning or by
drawing a picture which illuminates the meaning. These techniques use the right hand
side of the brain which is less often used in language activities. Some students respond
very well to using artistic or imaginative approaches. Sometimes a group might be
encouraged to produce pictures, illustrated words or words shaped for meaning.
These can then be shared in the group. Sometimes the images produced help **other**
students to remember particularly difficult words.

3 | The Role of Dictation

Purposes:

- To help students relate the spoken and written forms of language.

- To ensure that they practise the writing of words.

- To ensure that words are placed in context.

- To enable the tutor to identify common mistakes of the student and provide practice opportunities.

- Enables a group to tackle the same passage which may address a variety of needs.

- Provides opportunity for writing practice whilst providing constant support and opportunities for feedback.

- Can provide pre-test and test material.

- Can be functional or fun or both.

Preparing a dictation

A dictation should never be too long. It is unlikely ever to match a real situation which the student will encounter. You will usually use it to test words that have been learned, to provide writing practice for the student and to enable you to see how your student tackles writing words they are not really sure about.

It may be most appropriate to use something that the student wrote previously. This will ensure that language, vocabulary and content match the student's purposes. If you decide to compose something yourself it is important that you use the student's language.

You may have a routine which includes a dictation on a regular basis. You will always want to be sure that the student understands the purposes of the dictation and the procedures which will be used. Explain the content of the piece and then read it through in its entirety before reading it phrase by phrase.

When students have finished writing they should read through and decide if they want to make any changes. How the dictation is marked will depend on the nature of the class and the stage that the student has reached. You may:

- suggest that students mark the work themselves from a master copy

- get students to mark one another's work in pairs
- take the work away for marking at another time.

You will need to be sure that the marking matches the purposes. If the piece has been designed to test specific words or letter strings, these are the items which should be commented on unless the student is insistent upon being told about other possible errors.

4 | Spelling and Accreditation

Many students like to work towards accreditation for the literacy skills which they develop. You may be teaching such a student or your may encourage your student to think about accreditation. You will certainly want the student to see improvement in spelling as part of a wider development of literacy skills. Participating in an accredited programme has the additional advantage of ensuring that the student does engage in a wide range of literacy activities and does not limit their efforts to just spelling.

The City & Guilds Certificate 3793 (**Wordpower**) offers four levels of achievement and accreditation.

With reference to spelling:

Foundation level requires the student to check and correct spelling sufficiently for writing to be understood by the intended reader; in short, simple letters or notes.

Foundation level also requires the student to fill in simple forms or formats though no mention of spelling is made in this context.

However, even at this level encouraging accuracy of spelling is very important. The words required are likely to be in the personally important vocabulary of the student. As such they will be required repeatedly. Correct spelling at this stage provides the sound foundation for good spelling in more complicated pieces of writing.

Stage One requires the student to check and correct spelling sufficiently to maintain the confidence of the intended reader. This is in letters, reports and messages containing several ideas.

This is an important developmental stage for the improving speller. At Foundation level it is possible to concentrate on the spelling of individual words which have been identified as crucial for the learner in a limited writing context. At Stage One the flow of the writing becomes important. At this stage it is anticipated that students can write the correct spellings in context whilst concentrating on the meaning of the text. From your point of view this means providing lots of opportunities and reasons for the student to **use** words learned in sustained pieces of writing. The proof reading required is also of a different order as now the words which might be spelt incorrectly are embedded in continuous prose. At this stage particularly you must avoid the student thinking that spelling is the most important aspect of their writing. Encourage the student to check that pieces which they have written express their ideas and intentions accurately and well. It is only then that they should concentrate on surface features like spelling and punctuation.

Stages Two and **Three** each demand that the student use spelling appropriate for the audience and purpose.

Spelling is either right or wrong. It is one skill of writing which requires conformity and exactness. These higher levels reflect the writer's growing confidence. What is expected is that the writer will select words for their cogency and never because they are easy to spell. The task of tutors is to help students to widen the horizons of their reading and writing and to extend their writing vocabulary so that they choose words for elegance and power.

Stages in the development of spelling

Foundation:

- Can distinguish and recognise significant letter strings.
- Personally important words.
- Common words.
- Meaningful letter strings.
- Can reproduce in writing without copying these words and letter strings.
- Can proof read for spelling errors in short pieces which they have written.
- Can correct such errors.

Stage One:

- Will use language which they wish to use without worrying about spelling.
- Can proof read longer pieces of text in order to produce correct spelling.
- Having identified an error can use a wide range of strategies for dealing with it.

Stages Two and Three:

- Can produce pieces of writing for a range of purposes without significant spelling errors.

5 | Aids and Resources

The resources which you are able to use and choose to use as aids in teaching spelling will depend very largely on the context in which you are teaching and the particular preferences of the student.

Flash cards

Before you make any teaching materials check what's available at the centre where you are employed. Commercially produced materials are likely to be better visually than those you produce yourself though it is important to look for things which are directly relevant and useful to your student.

It is useful to have available flash cards of the most common English words. These can be used for spelling and for handwriting practice. You might also find that it is worth making cards of some of the words which are most commonly mis-spelt. If you teach several students you will find the same words cropping up repeatedly.

If you are teaching a specialist subject you will find it useful to prepare flash cards for the technical vocabulary which will be required.

Everyday material

The greatest help to the speller is the written language which they will see around them, particularly that which provides examples of the sorts of things which they need or want to write. It follows that you will have available forms, letters, stories, CV's, course notes, etc., as appropriate to the needs of the student. In many cases students themselves should be able to provide these. Students are in any case the best source of such material. Where students are on college courses, text books or lists of equipment will similarly be used.

Spelling books

There are plenty of books around which provide suggestions for activities which will improve spelling. It is important that students can access these for themselves and that they know it is important to focus on the work which has been identified in their action plan. It is **not** helpful for them to work through a book from page to page without a clear plan.

Worksheets

If you are working in an educational institution, you will probably have a variety of resources at your disposal. These are likely to include worksheets. If they are well produced and well organised you may well find some that meet the specific needs of your student. However you will no doubt also find gaps and need to make some yourself. There are some guiding principles in producing worksheets for spelling development:

- **Readability** – all worksheets should be clear, self-explanatory, well laid out and without too much information on any sheet.

- The student should be given the encouragement and opportunity to **write**. If you feel it is beneficial for the student to write a **part** of a word, always structure the worksheet so that writing a part of a word is followed by the requirement to write the **whole** word.

- Students need to write the word in an appropriate context. This may mean providing forms for completion, or stimulating the writing of continuous prose.

- Words should never be **copied**. It is most important that they are written from **memory**.

- Worksheets should be designed to encourage self-checking and self-access.

- Don't think, or allow your student to think, that having spelt a word correctly on a worksheet means that it has been learned. Only if the word is used in context in a real situation regularly can it be assumed that it has been learned.

Technological aids

Use of Computers/Wordprocessors

Whether your student will use a computer or word processor will depend on what's available in the classroom and in the home. If the student habitually uses a word processor you will want to do so in class.

If the student has no access to a word processor at home or work you will need to take account of the differences between spelling in handwriting and using a keyboard. There are circumstances where you may try to secure the use of a word processor for your students:

- if the student has a physical disability which makes handwriting difficult or impossible

- if they have firmly ingrained habits of illegible writing

- if they feel that using a word processor confers some status or credibility to what they are doing

- if they need to produce high quality text and seem to be unlikely to achieve it in their own handwriting.

If they use a word processor in class but have no access to one at home, they will need to be encouraged to produce some handwritten work in class if they are to practise sufficiently to make improvements in their spelling.

Word processors are useful tools for spelling particularly as they utilise the visual and motor skills most needed for spelling.

There are spelling programmes available for wordprocessors and computers (see *Basic Skills Software Guide*, ALBSU, 1991).

Aids which reduce the strain

Planning ahead
During the planning of a piece of writing encourage your student to identify some of the vocabulary which they might want to use. It is helpful for the student to have already written down words which would otherwise cause problems.

Reference card
Encourage your student to carry a reference list or card or book with words that they may need to write at home or work. This will enable them to check spellings of words which they feel might make them vulnerable particularly in public situations. It's also a good way of encouraging students to practise.

Prepared texts
Enable students to produce CVs, etc., in class if they are likely to need to refer to the content in order to fill in forms or letters of application.

Encourage students to make lists of topic-related words which they might want to use, e.g. numbers for cheque writing, lists of ingredients if they are on a catering course, or tools if they are on a construction course.

A Thesaurus

Did you know that thesaurus just means a treasure? (the two words come from the same root). You will provide some of the treasures which will enhance learning, for instance reference books such as commercially produced thesauruses. In addition to such printed word lists, the student is likely to find individual word collections particularly useful. But only if such lists are readily accessible and easily usable. This means that they must be arranged in ways which suit the needs of the student.

The categories which are used should, therefore, be devised by the student and will depend upon their individual purposes for writing.

Lists might be categorised according to a students main study area, e.g. catering or might relate to every day functional tasks like writing cheques or words for applications. They could also be categorised according to their derivations, e.g. words from the arabic, or by visual pattern.

It is particularly useful if students categorise words in a variety of ways. Doing so will help them to see inter-connections and relationships. **'Phone'** for example might be listed as:

- ph words
- words from the greek
- words for technology
- 'one' words
- words to do with sound.

Students who think up such categories and use them will begin to notice for themselves that *ph* words in the English language are likely to come from a Greek root; that *phone* indicates the meaning 'sound'; that English borrows extensively from Greek for technological words.

Electronic aids

There are numerous electronic spelling aids on the market. If any are available to you or your students it is a good idea to test them out. Most of them incorporate a variety of advantages and disadvantages. They may be very helpful for some students. The newly available *Roget's thesaurus* for example has the disadvantage of encouraging the student to enter even a bizarre version of the spelling of a word.

However, it has the advantage of:

- being easily portable, clearly adult and of providing accurate spelling of 80,000 words
- specifying the grammatical function of the word and of providing synonyms, antonyms and idioms
- being able to search for words containing specific letter strings
- including games such as **hangman** which can be played at different levels
- providing autonomy for students who want to check a spelling for themselves before putting pen to paper or even just out of interest.

Checklist for aids

- Is the aid perceived as **adult**?
- Is it easy to **use**?
- Is it easy to **read**?
- Is it easy to **understand**?
- Is it easy to **carry around**?
- Does the student **like** it?
- Can the student see a **need for it**?

Games

Specific games are described in the sections on teaching methods:

1. Hangman.
2. How many words can you write that contain the letter string.
3. What letter string will complete this word *(see Example No.9)*.
4. Crosswords/wordtowers/wordsearch.
   Make up some which focus on particular letter strings.

Example No.9

Complete the table below, using the letter string 'and'.

After each definition write the word in full without looking at the first column.

br___ ___ ___ y	– an alcoholic drink	....
c___ ___ ___ y	– a sweet	....
d___ ___ ___ y	– in fine fettle!	....
g___ ___ ___ er	– a male goose	....
h___ ___ ___ y	– skilful	....
isl___ ___ ___	– a piece of land surrounded by water	....
dem___ ___ ___	– a forceful request	....
comm___ ___ ___	– a forceful instruction	....
p___ ___ ___ a	– an animal from China	....
qu___ ___ ___ ary	– a dilemma	....
s___ ___ ___ y	– covered in sand	....

Now use each word in a sentence.

5. Write down as many foodstuffs/countries/rivers/etc. as you can that begin with a 'b' etc.

6. You can use **any** game which involves the production of **whole words**. There are many available commercially:

- Scrabble

- Boggle, etc.

Useful resources – for tutors

You will find useful:

- Strips of paper ready for the writing of spellings.

- Own notebook to record spellings in an organised form.

- Action plan sheets.

- Diagnostic sheets.

- Flash cards.

- Pens of different colours and thicknesses.

- Snopake or similar.

- Scissors.

- Paste.

- Good dictionary with large print.

- Range of dictionaries, encyclopaedias, thesauruses, etc.

6 | Using and Choosing a Dictionary

Encourage your students to use their own dictionary regularly. If your student is not in the habit of using a dictionary, you may need to teach dictionary skills. The dictionary is not the best place to refer to initially if you are trying to find out how a word is spelt unless the speller has a pretty good idea of the spelling in the first place. Dictionaries are most useful for checking on the meanings of words we're not sure about. But students are usually perfectly clear about the meanings of words which they mis-spell.

Using dictionaries

It is important that you have available and regularly use a dictionary yourself. By seeing you use a dictionary your student is much more likely to develop the habit.

You will need to ensure that a range of dictionaries is available in class.

The dictionary needs to be a constant source of information and delight.

To be a successful speller your student needs to feel confident with language, be able to **recollect** the way words look and be able to **work out** how a word should look.

The dictionary can help with all of these functions but not through students looking to see how a word is spelt.

The dictionary is more useful:

As a friend

Use games and activities to familiarise your student with a dictionary, its layout and various uses.

As a source of information

Students need to develop their knowledge of English. They will do this through usage, through interaction with other students, through your knowledge and through your teaching. To support this they need to be able to check on how words arrived at their current meanings and spellings. It is crucial therefore that students have access to good etymological information and can use it.

As a reference point

Your student can check grammar, pronunciation and sometimes even spelling.

Choosing a dictionary

There are numerous types of dictionary available, some specifically targeting those with spelling difficulties.

Your student will gain greatest benefit from having access to a range of different dictionaries but needs to own and regularly use one with which they feel most at home. They may want your guidance in choosing one. The guidance they need mirrors the considerations which you will take into account in selecting dictionaries for your own use.

Specific purpose

For most people, using a standard traditional dictionary is likely to be the most useful. Dictionaries which include examples of **mis-spellings** should not be used. It is better for the development of good spelling for students to see words **correctly** spelled.

Number of words included

Dictionaries which contain a limited number of words may seem like a useful option for adults with limited reading skills. But this is a false assumption. Even those who have reading difficulties are likely to have a spoken vocabulary of around 12,000 words. The number of words which they understand is likely to be larger than this. They need a dictionary which also includes new words which they may encounter through conversation, reading or study. A dictionary with at least 20,000 words is therefore necessary for the average student.

Layout

Dictionaries usually include a great deal of information. This information can be impenetrable, particularly for those less confident with literacy. You may wish to ensure that there are dictionaries available which limit the amount and type of information presented.

Relevance

You need to check that the dictionary contains the words which the student actually wants to refer to. Dictionaries which have a limited number of entries may not be useful for someone on a course which has a specialised vocabulary. Such students may want to look up technological terms. They will soon become frustrated if they look up words and fail to find them. A good homework exercise for students is for them to make a list of words in which they are interested and then to survey dictionaries in their local bookshop. They can compare notes afterwards. This critical reviewing of dictionaries is particularly important for students who may believe that dictionaries are somehow sacred and do not realise that there are bad ones and that even good ones may be unsuitable for their purpose.

Currency

Language develops all the time. The constant changes are reflected in the dictionary. Each new edition adds new words and includes altered definitions and usages. It may also jettison some which have become out-moded. It is very important that the dictionaries which students use reflect the current state of the language *(see Example Nos. 10, 11 and 12)*.

Example No.10

Getting to Know the Dictionary

Etymological Abbreviations

Dictionaries which contain etymological information usually use abbreviations which tell you from which language words come.

Look at the list of abbreviations below:

- guess to which language they refer

- write your guess on the right hand side

- check your answers in the dictionary

- find examples of words from each language

- write the words in sentences.

Amer.	**Ar.**
Austr.	**Braz.**
Chin.	**Dan.**
Du.	**Fr.**
Ger.	**Gr.**
It.	**Jap.**
M.E.	**Norw.**
O.B.	**Port.**

Dictionary Worksheet
<u>SIGN . . .</u>

Look up the word 'SIGN' in the dictionary.

In your own words write below what the word means:

_____

_____

_____

What languages does the word come from?

_____

_____

_____

Use the dictionary to write down six words which contain the word 'SIGN'. Write the meaning – in your own words – beside each one.

_____

_____

_____

_____

Practise the spellings of the 'SIGN' words by using them to fill in the gaps below.

Each sentence should make sense. Do NOT copy the words, write them from memory then check them. JOIN your writing.

1. Please write your _____ on the dotted line.

2. I did it more by accident than by _____ .

3. The supervisor has _____ from her post.

4. There was a _____ number of applicants.

5. I acted as _____ to his will.

6. The traffic _____ were out of order.

Comprehension

Even if all the other features are right there is no point in having a dictionary available which students (or you) cannot understand because the definitions are written in difficult language, or because the definition contains another word that the student is unlikely to know.

Robustness

In the hope that the dictionary will be subject to frequent usage, you will want to be sure that it can cope. Check that it will readily open up fully for detailed perusal.

Print size

The smaller the print the greater the visual burden placed upon the reader. White space can be very beneficial for the reader. You will need to ensure therefore that there are dictionaries available with a size of print and a pattern of spacing which makes the text as readable as possible.

You may also have students who need a specifically large print dictionary because of visual impairment.

Example No.12

Getting to Know the Dictionary

Look up the following words in the dictionary:

port	sherry
madeira	calvados
gin	tequila
champagne	chianti

From which language did we get the words?

What do the words have in common?

Discuss your thoughts with your tutor or another student.
Use each word in a sentence.

Write an account of an incident which requires as many of these words as possible.

Describe a party using as many of the words as possible.

---

7 | Special Problems

This handbook is addressed to tutors who are dealing with students who do not have serious educational problems. However, some students who want to improve their spelling could have additional problems which get in the way of successful learning. You will need to be able to spot some of these difficulties and find ways of helping students with them. It is sensible to seek further advice. There are specialist publications by ALBSU and other specialist bodies that can provide help.

Visual problems

The problem

If students have problems with their eyesight.

Towards solutions

- Encourage them to use any aids which have been prescribed for them.
- Encourage them to sit in a part of the room which give them the best view of aids which you are using.
- Use large print it if helps.
- Encourage them to sit in positions which give the best view of any reading materials.
- They will need to avoid clutter which might confuse the visual field, e.g. they need to keep writing surfaces clear and to use clean sheets of paper for new tasks.
- Encourage such students to experiment with different colours and sizes of writing to discover what is most effective for them.

Visual perception

The problem

If diagnostic sheets reveal that a student's spelling errors consistently cluster in **additions, omissions or transpositions,** e.g. *persissteence, quanty, coulors.*

Towards solutions

It may indicate that they need much more practice in visual discrimination and visual memory.

Visual discrimination

You can prepare sheets with appropriate words. Ask the student to identify differences; mark differences; trace over distinctive parts of the word; write the words or parts of words as a gap filling exercise.

Students who have even more severe problems may need to do some shape discrimination.

You can make any of these activities into games. The overhead projector is a particularly useful aid since you can expose the words for a chosen amount of time. The student may need to work slowly at first but needs to be encouraged to speed up. Eventually the discriminations need to be made literally in a flash.

Visual memory

Again the overhead projector is a useful aid. But you can use flash cards if you have no access to an 'ohp'.

- Show the letter string.
- Switch off or turn over.
- Ask the student to write the letter string down.
- Show the correct version.
- Ask the student to proof read.
- Explore any discrepancies in detail using multi-sensory approaches.

The more difficulty the student has in doing this successfully, the more you will need to intensify the sensory input so that the student can 'see' the visual pattern.

Hearing

The problem

Some students will tell you that they have hearing problems.

Towards solutions

- Encourage them to use aids prescribed for them.

- Encourage them to sit in the part of the room which gives them the greatest advantage (you may additionally need to consider the acoustics of the room in case there is a better alternative).

- Try to face the student when you are speaking.

- Encourage other members of the class to do the same.

- Encourage the student to let you know immediately if they feel that they are missing anything.

The problem

Some students will appear to have a hearing problem which they have not mentioned or acknowledged.

Towards solutions

Encourage them to seek help from a specialist if you really think that they need it.

Auditory discrimination

The problem

If students appear to have difficulty distinguishing between similar sounds, e.g.

cot / cut

dam / damp

collapse / collapsed.

Towards solutions

You will need to ensure that they take particular note of the *look* of the word. Students can also use *linguistic information* and *knowledge of serial probability* to decide on correct spellings, e.g. work on tenses can help students to know when 'ed' is required even if they do not usually hear the distinction.

Motor skills

The problem

Good spelling, as we have seen, requires fluent, confident writing. Students who have poor motor skills are, therefore, at a disadvantage.

Towards solutions

If there are long-standing physical reasons for lack of motor skills it may be best to use electronic aids like wordprocessors and computers which require less fluidity of motion.

Students who have habitually produced poor-looking writing are usually absolutely delighted the first time that they produce something legible and adult looking. You may find that a wordprocessor can be made available in the classroom or is available in an adjacent classroom. Nowadays typewriters are usually very easy to come by and some students with motor difficulties find them very useful.

Letter formation

The problem

Some students produce very untidy and illegible writing as a camouflage for their poor spelling. Some do so because the have never learned correct letter formation.

Towards solutions

It is very important that these students learn to form letters with speed and confidence. Style of handwriting will develop alongside these qualities.

Memory

The problem

It is most frustrating for those who want to improve their spelling to find that words which they got right in their spelling test last week are now completely eluding them or appearing with the same spelling mistake which they made originally. This can be frustrating for you too.

Towards solutions

It is important for students and tutors alike to realise that it is only **frequent, repeated practice** of a word written **fluently** that will establish its spelling permanently in long-term memory. This motor practice needs to be augmented with the **noticing** of features of the word.

It is also important that the memory is not **overloaded**. The number of new words to be learned should never be more than about 7 in any one week. But the words chosen need to be practised and written over and over again.

This learning needs to be in the framework of a planned programme so that the student can see how much it is reasonable to expect to achieve. Handwriting developed as part of the spelling programme thus reduces the learning load.

Remember that **copying** cuts through the system, relying only on short-term memory. It avoids the use of the long-term memory which is the key to successful spelling development.

Problems you cannot deal with

You are trying to help students with spelling. Sometimes you may encounter students who have serious problems or problems which you feel you are not competent to deal with. In such cases always be ready to ask for guidance from your manager. **Do not try to deal with problems which are outside your sphere of competence.**

8 | Sample Worksheet

Here is an example of the type of worksheet which you might produce for your student. It is based on the word **end**. You could substitute any letter string which has been identified as important for your student to work on.

END

- look at the word
- cover it
- now write it from memory
- uncover the word and check that you have spelt it correctly

Think of other words which contain 'end'.

Write down as many as you can think of.

Ask a tutor or another student if they can think of any more.

Write them down.

Put each word which you have written into a sentence.

Write the sentence down.

See if you can write something which contains as many words as possible which contain 'end'.

Write the word WITH YOUR EYES CLOSED.

Are you happy with the way it looks?

If not try again.

Look up 'end' in the dictionary.

How did this word come into the English language?

Can you think of a word which has the same meaning as '**end**'?

Write the word '**end**' in your word book together with any other '**end**' words which you think will be useful in the end!

For homework:

Look out for words containing 'end'.

Write them in your notebook.

Write them into sentences.

Write something with as many 'end' words as possible.

9 | Summary: What the Curriculum Needs to Include

Skills your students will need

Reading

Your student needs to be as confident and as fluent as possible in reading. Reading a lot will help (not to 'spot' spellings but to enrich language in a much more general sense).

Proof reading

Unless your student can spot their own mistakes they are unlikely to make much progress.

Handwriting or keyboard skills

All research findings stress the important role of the actual writing – 'feeling' the word being written is an important aid to memory.

Knowledge of the language

A good spelling programme will build up a thorough and enthusiastic knowledge of language.

Attentive behaviour

If students don't learn to **notice** and **categorise** features of the language they are unlikely to improve their spelling.

Visualisation

The poor speller is likely to have poor skills of visualisation but needs to develop them as much as possible.

The vocabulary of spelling

Learning the words which define the spelling process will aid their thinking about it.

Strategies for learning spelling

Students need to develop strategies which suit their own learning styles but should include:

- **Visual**
- **Auditory**
- **Kinaesthetic**
- **Logical.**

Systematic recording or learning

The student needs to see how each activity in the learning programme builds towards **mastery** of spelling. It is necessary therefore that each step is recorded and used to prompt extensive practice and further success.

Activities you will need to incorporate:

Learning

Providing the input which will enable the student to learn initially.

Repetition

Effective learning means **over-learning**. You will need to ensure that the student understands the need for repetition.

Spaced learning

You will understand, as the student may not initially, the need for relearning at intervals.

Multi-sensory presentation

Students who have found spelling a problem need the stimulus of learning through every sense. You will want to be sure that students know **why**. This is the best way to motivate them.

Context

Always make sure that spelling is taught in a proper context and not in isolation.